COTTONMOUTHS

AMAZING SNAKES

Ted O'Hare

Rourke
Publishing LLC
Vero Beach, Florida 32964

www.rourkepublishing.com

PHOTO CREDITS: All photos © Lynn M. Stone expect pp. 12, 15
© George Van Horn

Title page: *The Florida cottonmouth is one of three types of cottonmouths in the United States.*

Editor: Frank Sloan

Cover and interior design by Nicola Stratford

Library of Congress Cataloging-in-Publication Data

O'Hare, Ted, 1961-
  Cottonmouths / Ted O'Hare.
     p. cm. -- (Amazing snakes)
  Includes bibliographical references and index.
  ISBN 1-59515-146-X (hardcover)
  1. Agkistrodon piscivorus--Juvenile literature. I. Title. II. Series: O'Hare, Ted, 1961- Amazing snakes.
  QL666.O69O42 2004
  597.96'38--dc22
                              2004008017

Printed in the USA

CG/CG

table of contents

cottonmouths

Cottonmouths are relatives of rattlesnakes. Like all snakes, cottonmouths are **reptiles**. They are **venomous** snakes and members of the *Crotalidae* family.

Unlike many of their relatives, they like to live in freshwater **habitats**.

One of the cottonmouth's closest relatives is the Mexican moccasin, also known as Taylor's cantil, shown here.

The name cottonmouth comes from the white lining in the snake's mouth.

where they Live

Did you Know?

Cottonmouths have been known to live for 20 years.

Cottonmouths live in the swamps, lakes, rivers, and marshes of the southeastern United States. They like to lie in the warm sun near water. If their habitats dry up, they will travel great distances to find water once more.

The Big Cypress Swamp in southwest Florida is ideal cottonmouth habitat.

Did you Know?

The cottonmouth may be 4 to 5 feet (1.2 to 1.5 meters) long.

What They Look Like

Cottonmouths have scales. These may be olive, brown, and black, and they have ridges. Some types have bands that are dark brown with a light color on each side of the bands. Some cottonmouths are a solid dark color. A dark band runs from each eye to the corner of the mouth.

The western cottonmouth is a third type of cottonmouth.

Another type of cottonmouth is the eastern cottonmouth, coiling to strike in this picture.

their senses

The cottonmouth's tongue reaches out to bring in particles. The **Jacobson's organ** in the roof of the snake's mouth analyzes these particles.

The sense of smell is helped by sight and heat. The cottonmouth is able to see moving **prey**. And the **heat receptor pits** on the face sense the prey's warmth.

A cottonmouth's forked tongue helps it study nearby objects and movements.

Nostril

Heat receptor pit

Fangs in sheaths

Tongue

Windpipe

The Head and Mouth

The head of the cottonmouth has a flat top. Hollow fangs are folded against the roof of its mouth. When the snake bites, the fangs extend. They inject **venom** from the venom gland into the prey.

A close-up of a cottonmouth's head shows the snake's fangs and heat receptors.

The jaws stretch so the snake can swallow whole animals. The windpipe extends from the throat to the front of the mouth. This lets the snake breathe while it is swallowing prey.

A cottonmouth begins to swallow a fish, a favorite prey.

Baby Cottonmouths

The mother snake gives birth to 5 to 15 babies in late summer or early fall. The babies are about 10 inches (25 centimeters) long. When it is born, the baby cottonmouth has bright patterns with bands and a yellow tail. As it grows older, the patterns fade, and the snake becomes darker.

Did you know?
As soon as it is born, a cottonmouth is able to kill small prey.

A baby Florida cottonmouth begins to shed its first skin.

their Prey

Cottonmouths often hunt in water, but they also look for animals on land.

Because cottonmouths are good swimmers, they often hunt for prey in water. Fish, frogs, ducks, and small turtles are good prey. The cottonmouth also eats other snakes. The cottonmouth attacks its prey with a quick, venomous bite and swallows it at once.

Alligators attack and eat cottonmouths, but cottonmouths sometimes return the favor by eating baby alligators!

Did you Know?

Alligators, birds, and raccoons eat the cottonmouth.

their Defense

Cottonmouths avoid enemies whenever possible. If it cannot escape, the cottonmouth shows its fangs and the white lining of its mouth. It shakes its tail to warn the enemy that it is in danger. If the enemy comes too close, the cottonmouth will strike.

An angry western cottonmouth warns enemies to keep their distance.

The cottonmouth's diamond-shaped head helps separate it from the many non-venomous water snakes of North America.

cottonmouths and People

Because they like water, cottonmouths often hide in fishing boats. But if they sense people, cottonmouths will race to get back in the water.

The bite of the cottonmouth is painful. It can cause swelling and damage tissue near the bite.

Glossary

habitats (HAB uh tatz) — Special places where plants and animals live

heat receptor pits (HEET ree CEP tur PITZ) — parts of a snake's face, which give the snake information about the size and location of its prey

Jacobson's organ (JAYK ub sunz ORG un) — the part of a snake that analyzes a scent the snake has picked up

prey (PRAY) — animals hunted and killed by other animals for food

reptiles (REP TYLZ) — animals with cold blood, a backbone, and scales or plates

venom (VEN um) — poisonous matter that some snakes use to injure or kill prey

venomous (VEN uh muss) — containing poisonous matter

index

Further Reading

Feldman, Heather. *Cottonmouths*. PowerKids, 2004
Solway, Andrew. *Deadly Snakes*. Heinemann Library, 2004
Wechsler, Doug. *Pit Vipers*. PowerKids, 2001

Websites to Visit

www.enchantedlearning.com/subjects/reptiles/snakes/printouts.shtml
www.flmnh.ufl.edu/natsci/herpetology/fl-guide/venomsnk.htm
www.42explore.com/snake2.htm

About the Author

Ted O'Hare is an author and editor of children's nonfiction books. He divides his time between New York City and a home upstate.